KILLER CREATURES

SHARK

DAVID JEFFERIS
AND
TONY ALLAN

Belitha Press

First published in the UK in 2001 by
Belitha Press
An imprint of Chrysalis Books plc
64 Brewery Road, London N7 9NT

Paperback edition first published
in 2002

© David Jefferis / Tony Allan 2001

Design and editorial production:
 Alpha Communications
Educational advisor: Julie Stapleton
Picture research: Kay Rowley

ISBN 1 84138 301 5 (hardback)
ISBN 1 84138 380 5 (paperback)

British Library Cataloguing in
Publication Data for this book is
available from the British Library.

Printed in Hong Kong

10 9 8 7 6 5 4 3 2 1

Acknowledgements
We wish to thank the following
individuals and organizations for
their help and assistance and for
supplying material in their
collections:
Alpha Archive, Ardea London Ltd,
V. Audet/Sunset, Franco Banfi,
BBC Natural History Unit, Mark
Bowle, Bruce Coleman Collection,
Mark Conlin, FLPA, Fuji film,
Michael Glover, Howard Hall, Charles
and Sandra Hood, Rudie Kuitner,
Yves Lefevre, NHPA Natural History
Photographic Agency,
Oxford Scientific Films, Pacific Stock,
Gavin Page, Doug Perrine, Planet
Earth Pictures, Jeff Rotman, Marty
Snyderman, Still Pictures, Valerie
Taylor, DP Wilson, Norbert Wu

▲ Divers swim with a whale shark.
It feeds on tiny sea animals, so it is
no danger to humans. When a shark
swallowed a diver by accident, it
coughed him up before he was hurt!

CONTENTS

LOOK FOR THE SHARK BOX

Look for the little black shark in boxes like this.
Here you will find extra shark facts, stories
and other interesting information!

OCEAN HUNTERS

Sharks are among the fiercest hunters in the sea. They have no enemies to threaten them, except other sharks and humans.

▲ Here are three of the weird-looking sharks that swam in the oceans millions of years ago.

Sharks have been around for a very long time. Scientists think that the shark family goes back 350 million years or more. Early types of shark were swimming around long before dinosaurs existed.

Today, there are at least 350 different kinds, or species, of shark. The biggest sharks can grow as big as a school bus. Others are full-grown at no more than 25 cm – you could lay one on this page, with room to spare.

Most sharks spend their time roaming the seas. A few species live mostly on the ocean floor, lying in wait for unwary prey to come close.

◀ This photographer stays inside a steel cage for protection, in case a shark decides to bite!

🦈 DEADLY TO HUMANS?

Sharks have a fearsome reputation, but attacks on humans are rare. Even so, sharks need to be treated with care, as they are mostly meat-eaters. If a shark feels trapped, or mistakes a human for its normal prey, then it may move in and take a bite.

▼ The great white shark is
probably the most dangerous
shark today. An adult may weigh
more than 20 men, and its teeth
are longer than your hand!

SHARKS ARE DIFFERENT

Sharks may look like typical fish, with fins for movement and gills for breathing. But in some ways, they are very different from other fish.

▲ The basking shark can stay at the surface with only a slow forward motion. A large, oily liver helps the shark keep afloat.

Most fish have balloon-like swim bladders that help them control their depth in the water. A shark doesn't have this, so it has to keep swimming, otherwise it sinks slowly to the sea-bed. Instead of bone, a shark's skeleton is made of gristle-like cartilage, like human ears. Cartilage is softer and bendier than bone, which allows a shark to twist and turn easily.

► Like all sharks, the gulf catshark from South Australia has denticles, instead of scales.

the catshark is unusual, because it has no tall 'shark' fin

Unlike most fish, sharks have no scales. A shark's skin is made up of tiny, sharp denticles. These point backwards, so if you stroke shark skin from head to tail it feels smooth. Rub the other way, and it is rough as sandpaper. Sailors in the old days often used shark skin to scrub the wooden decks of sailing ships.

SHARK RELATIVES

The closest relatives of the shark are skates and rays – strange, flattened-out fish that also have skeletons made of cartilage. The sting ray is a favourite food of the hammerhead shark. Hammerheads don't seem to mind the ray's sharp tail. Many have been seen swimming along with a dozen or more stings stuck in their mouths, like porcupine quills.

◄ No one knows exactly why the hammerhead shark has such an oddly-shaped head. Its wide-set eyes may help it to judge distances accurately.

STRANGE SHARKS

There are many shark species, and some of them look very strange. Among the oddest are the horn sharks and wobbegongs.

▲ The Port Jackson horn shark takes its name from a bay in Australia. Rows of small teeth grind up shellfish.

Horn sharks have spines that stick up on either side of the dorsal (top) fins. But it is the snout that looks weird. A horn shark looks more like a pig than a fish! Big nostrils give the shark a good sense of smell, useful for sniffing out foods such as shellfish and sea urchins.

There are eight species of horn sharks. They mostly grow less than 1.5m long and live in shallow waters in the Pacific and Indian Oceans.

▼ A baby swell shark emerges from its egg case. This shark will spend most of its life on, or near, the sea bed.

WHAT ARE GILLS?

Gills are the body organs which fish use to breathe. Bony fish have a gill cover on each side of their heads. Most sharks have five gill slits each side. To breathe, a shark takes a mouthful of water, then squeezes it out through the slits. The gills take oxygen gas from the water. The oxygen is dissolved in the blood and pumped around the body by the heart.

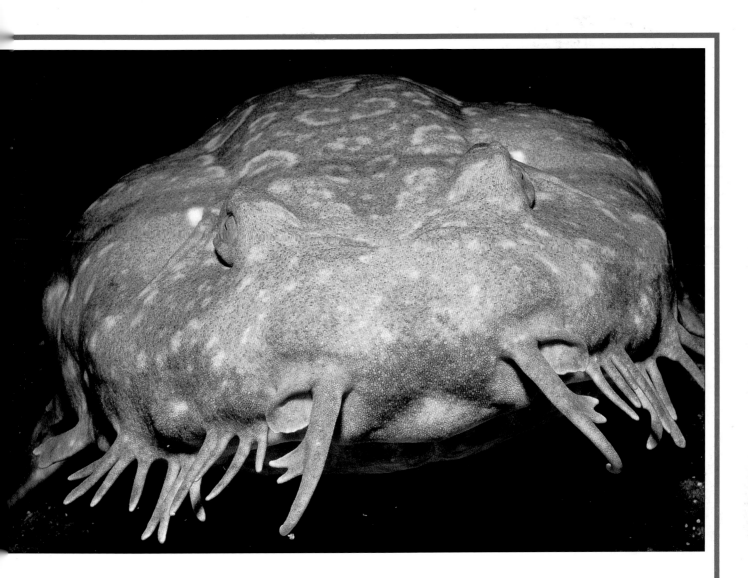

The wobbegong hardly looks like a shark at all, with its flattened body, and eyes on the top of the head. It spends most of its time on the sea bed, in shallow water. The wobbegong's main weapon is camouflage. It lies very still, until a fish or crab comes too close. Then, with a quick bite, the wobbegong snaps up its meal.

The swell shark also uses camouflage, while it waits for prey. If the swell shark is attacked, it closes its gill slits, swallows water and swells up, like a balloon. With luck, it wedges itself tight under a rock, to avoid being eaten.

▲ The wobbegong's strange 'beard' lets it hide among seabed plants. Wobbegongs live around the coasts of Asian countries and Australia.

EGGS OR PUPS?

Sharks have babies in two ways. Some sharks lay eggs, but most give birth to live young. Baby sharks are called pups or cubs.

Shark eggs are like leathery pouches. They protect the growing baby, or embryo. Inside the egg is a yolk. The embryo grows inside the case, feeding on the yolk, until it is ready to hatch. The mother shark leaves her eggs anchored to seaweed or rocks on the seabed.

You sometimes see empty eggs, washed ashore on beaches, where they are known as mermaid's purses. Sharks that lay eggs like this include the dogfish and swell shark.

◀ This enlarged picture shows a lesser spotted dogfish in its case, laid by the mother shark. The dogfish embryo will soon be ready to hatch out.

 **YOUNG AND OLD**

Sizes of shark litters vary widely – a hammerhead shark may give birth to up to 40 pups at a time, while lemon sharks have given birth to 17 pups.

Some sharks live for a long time. The great white shark can live for 30 to 35 years. The lemon shark has a lifespan of 75 years or more. A whale shark may live even longer, though no one knows for sure.

Lemon sharks are born live, in shallow lagoons, away from pounding waves. But whether they are born live or hatched from eggs, all pup sharks have to look after themselves from the start, as mother sharks leave their babies after the birth.

In the first few months, many pups are eaten by hungry sea creatures, such as barracuda or other sharks. A growing shark may stay in the same area for years, gradually exploring further away as it gets older.

▲ This Caribbean reef shark pup is hiding among the roots of mangrove trees.

▶ A lemon shark gives birth to a pup (arrowed). The pup is born tail-first, then the mother swims away.

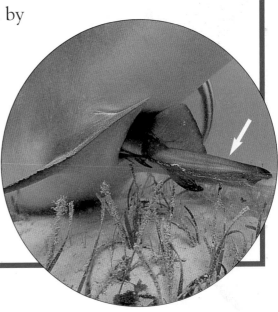

TRACKING PREY

Sharks target their prey silently, then close in for the kill. During the hunt, sharks use all the senses we have, plus two extra ones.

▲ A sand tiger shark, ready for lunch. It can detect one drop of blood in a million drops of water.

A shark often senses its prey first by hearing it, as sound can travel far and fast under water. For example, a shark might catch the sound of a seal near the surface.

From several hundred metres away, the shark is able to smell prey. An injured animal is easy to track, as a shark can sense tiny amounts of blood in the water.

Closer in, the shark sees its target. The shark may also be using one of its extra senses, called distant touch. This allows a shark to feel vibrations in the water, along a line down each side of its body.

▶ This closeup of a leopard shark shows the 'distant touch' line, marked by the arrow. The line goes from nose to tail, on both sides of the shark's body.

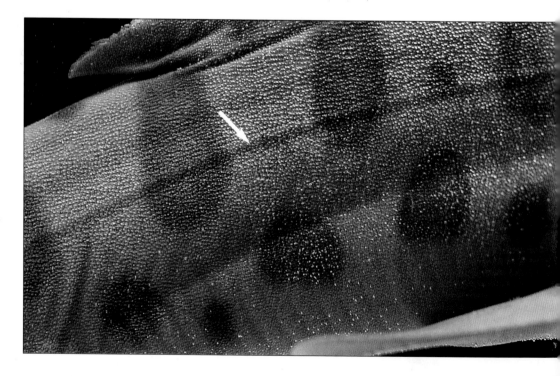

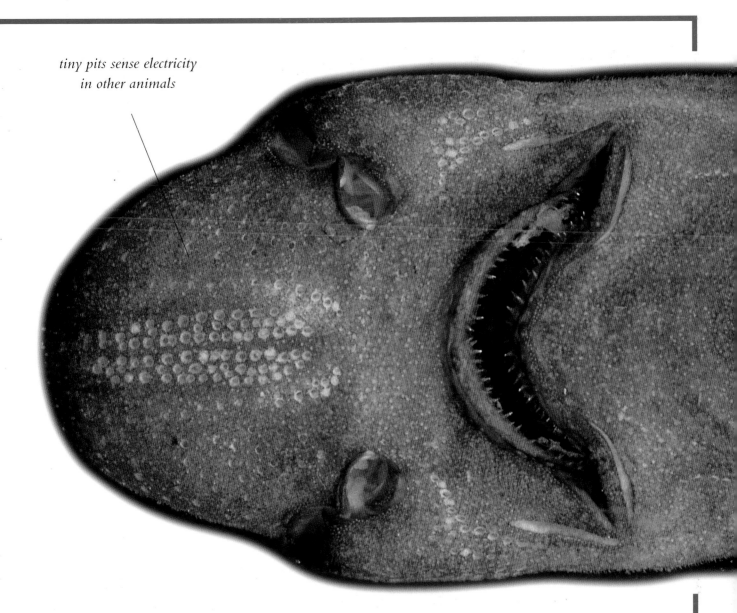

*tiny pits sense electricity
in other animals*

Closing in on the prey, the shark's other extra sense starts to work. Tiny pits in the shark's snout pick up electric charges from the prey's body. These are caused by moving muscles, but are too small for humans to feel. Big movements create more electricity, so struggling prey makes a stronger signal for the shark to track.

As the shark moves in to attack, it may close its eyes to protect them from harm. Then it strikes blind – but usually with deadly accuracy.

▲ A scary view, showing the underneath of a cat shark's snout. You can see its mouth, nostrils and the pattern of tiny pits that sense electricity.

FEEDING TIME

Different sharks like different kinds of food. Some eat tiny creatures too small to see, others feast on seals and big fish, even other sharks.

▲ A cookie-cutter shark's mouth is shaped like a biscuit. Cookie-cutters may not be large, but the sharp teeth can slice through armoured underwater cables.

Shark food includes all kinds of sea creatures. Bigger sharks prey on fish, octopus, squid, shellfish and turtles. A sea bird resting on the surface makes an easy target, too. Many experts think that when sharks attack people it is usually by mistake. From below, a human swimming, or paddling full-length on a surfboard, can be mistaken for an unusual seal.

The cookie-cutter shark snaps chunks out of other fish, leaving behind biscuit-shaped bite marks.

 EXTENDING JAWS

Unlike human jaws and teeth, those of a shark are not joined firmly to its head.

When a shark opens its mouth to bite, the upper teeth reach forward, like spikes. They fold back towards the stomach when the shark snaps its jaws shut.

Some sharks eat mostly shellfish. These sharks have flattened teeth for crushing and grinding, rather than sharply pointed teeth for tearing.

The prospect of a meal excites sharks, and when a group comes across a lot of food they sometimes go wild. The sharks lose control, biting and snapping at anything, including each other. This is called a feeding frenzy.

Hungry sharks are not fussy eaters. Objects found in dead sharks' stomachs have included wooden planks, oil drums, rubber tyres, even old overcoats!

▲ Caribbean reef sharks feast on a ball of bait. Human shark researchers watch them warily.

▼ A turtle makes a crunchy snack for a large shark.

GENTLE GIANTS

The biggest shark of all is as long as a tennis court, and weighs as much as a large truck.

The whale shark is not only the biggest shark – the record is 12.65m long – but it is also the world's largest fish.

Nearly everything about the whale shark is huge. The mouth is more than a metre wide, the tail fin nearly 4m high, and the skin is about 20 cm thick.

◄ The basking shark is the second-biggest shark, and is also a harmless plankton-eater. Its name comes from its habit of lying in the sun (or basking) near the surface. The basking shark grows 10m or more.

speckle pattern on upper surfaces

▼ A diver gets a close-up view of a whale shark. Thousands of litres of water go down the shark's throat each hour, as it cruises at a leisurely 4 km/h.

The whale shark's teeth are tiny – smaller than a human baby's toenails. This is because the whale shark does not bite or rip its prey.

Instead, it cruises along like a giant sieve, scooping food from the water. The food is mostly plankton, sea creatures so small that you can see many of them only under a microscope.

the killer whale is a mammal

FISH OR MAMMAL?

Don't confuse a whale shark with a whale. The whale shark is a fish, the whale is a mammal. Like humans, whales are warm-blooded, breathe air and feed their young with milk. Whales are thought to be a species that once lived on the land, but returned to the sea millions of years ago.

DEADLY KILLERS

▲ A tiger shark's teeth. The tiger is one of the most aggressive sharks, along with the great white shark, bull shark and oceanic white-tip.

Sharks that the experts agree are really dangerous to humans are known as killer sharks.

The teeth of killer sharks are razor-sharp. Some sharks, such as the tiger shark, have saw-like edges for cutting power. Teeth are replaced before they go blunt. As an old tooth drops out, a new one is ready to take its place.

Humans are not attacked often, even by the most-feared species.

TAKE CARE – THESE SHARKS BITE!

Attacks on humans may not be common, but three in ten attacks are fatal, often through loss of blood. Sharks to avoid include the tiger shark, bull shark, ocean white-tip and the great white shark. There are many reports of bites and nips from other species, so the best advice for anyone who wants a close-up view of sharks is, 'Be very careful…'

Attack numbers are not known exactly, but most experts think there are fewer than 100 attacks each year on humans. More people die from bee and wasp stings than shark attacks.

Sharks are such good hunters that some fish, such as the remora, travel with them to live off the scraps they leave. Remoras are not attacked by the shark, because they carry out a useful job, cleaning off grubs and parasites.

▲ The remora has an oval sucker. This lets the remora stick to a shark for a free ride. The remora cleans the shark of parasites.

▼ The tiger shark is named for its stripes. They usually fade as the shark grows up. A remora is just under the shark's front fins.

GREAT WHITE SHARK

The great white shark is the deadliest killer of all sharks. It is also very large, growing up to 6.5m long – half as big again as a hippopotamus.

The great white's teeth are hard as steel and the huge jaws snap together in what may be the animal kingdom's strongest bite, though no one has yet worked out a way to measure it exactly.

▲ The huge jaws of a great white shark.

the tall dorsal fin is a typical feature of sharks

► This sea-lion just survived a great white shark attack. Great whites have eaten elephant seals weighing over two tonnes – more than a family car.

▼ The great white shark can swallow 45 kg of food at once. That's enough for it to live on for two months.

Great whites live mostly in tropical waters, though they have been spotted as far north as Britain and in the chilly seas around Antarctica. The Indian Ocean is a favourite cruising spot, where a great white may travel 500 km a day in search of food. Prey include seals, sea-lions, large fish and penguins.

The great white may be dangerous, but the chances of seeing one are small. Only about three are caught each year in the western Atlantic Ocean and they usually avoid contact with people.

MEETING A KILLER

One in three reported shark attacks on humans involves great whites. Yet they are not always killers. When the French undersea explorer Jacques Cousteau came across one off the Cape Verde Islands, it stared at Cousteau and his dive-companions for a moment, then turned tail and fled.

SHARK RESEARCH

▲ A researcher inspects a young hammerhead shark. Its eyes are at either end of the head.

There is still much to learn about sharks, so researchers use a wide range of equipment to help. But first they must protect themselves against sharp teeth.

All sharks are unpredictable, and researchers and photographers have to guard against attacks. They often use special equipment, such as a steel cage. A diver is usually safe inside one, although sharks often attack cages, even when food is left as bait outside. Scientists think that the metal may give off small electric currents, similar to the ones sharks sense in their prey (see page 13).

Divers can also use a special suit, made of fine steel mesh. It looks like chain-mail armour, and protects against smaller sharks. But it gives no defence against the mighty jaws of a great white.

MYSTERY OF THE MEGAMOUTH

The plankton-eating megamouth shark is very rare. The first one was discovered in 1976, and by 1999 only 13 more had been seen, most of them in the Pacific Ocean.

At first, megamouth's eating habits were a mystery. Plankton live near the surface, yet the shark is a deep-water species, so how does it manage to eat? Scientists tracked a megamouth to see if they could find out. The answer was simple – the shark spends its days in deep water, then comes up to feed at night.

◄ Scientists inject a calming drug into a lemon shark. When it is quiet, the scientists can check how fast it grows. Sharks grow slowly, compared to many bony fish.

◄ A blue shark snaps at a researcher's arm. The steel suit protects him against a shark this size.

strong cage used in emergency

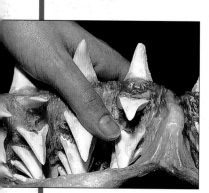

SHARKS AT RISK?

Some sharks are a threat to us, but most are no danger. Humans kill sharks in huge numbers for food, sport, or by accident.

▲ A great white shark's massive jaws are sold for up to £1000 in tourist souvenir shops.

▼ Two scientists carefully remove a fish hook from a tiger shark.

Sharks are hunted for lots of reasons. Many sharks are good to eat. The monkfish (a type of angel shark) is served in expensive restaurants, while rock salmon (dogfish shark) is served in fish-and-chip shops. In some countries shark-fin soup is very popular.

Shark skin is used for belts and clothing, while their teeth are used as jewellery. Liver oil taken from sharks is used in health pills and in anti-wrinkle cream.

Sport fishing is big business in many parts of the world, and great white sharks are often caught only for their jaws – the body may be left to rot.

▲ A tiger shark caught in a fishing net.

The biggest waste is killing sharks by mistake. Many sharks die when they are tangled in fishing nets. These deaths threaten some species, but the entire shark family is not in danger.

There is hope for sharks if humans stop seeing them only as a menace and look at sharks for the amazing creatures they are.

▲ Pills and potions are made from various shark parts.

 **A CURE FOR CANCER?**

Some medical researchers think that medicine made from shark cartilage may be useful in the fight against cancer in humans. Cartilage has few blood vessels, so it may act as a barrier, which could slow down the growth of a cancer.

Tests are being carried out, but at least one scientist says that shark cartilage is nothing special, and that cartilage from humans or chickens may have a similar effect. Hunting too many sharks for medical reasons could turn them into an endangered species.

SHARK FACTS

▼ The deep-sea goblin shark.

Here are some facts and stories about the world of sharks.

Deep-sea goblin

The goblin shark is one of the rarest sharks. It is weird looking with a long and pointed snout and tail. The goblin lives in deep water, perhaps down to 1200m.

Bellyful

One of the first people to write about great white sharks was a 16th-century professor. He reported that, 'a shark caught in the Mediterranean Sea was found to have the body of a man in armour in its belly.'

Sharks prefer men

Most shark attacks on humans happen in shallow water. Men are ten times more likely to be attacked than women, but nobody knows why.

Lazy eaters

Basking sharks are lazy eaters. They swim to the surface, then slowly sink, sieving plankton as they go. A basking shark filters more than 2000 tonnes of water an hour in this way.

Shark alley

The coasts of KwaZulu-Natal, South Africa, are the most shark-infested spots in the world. Swimmers mix with three dangerous shark species – the great white, tiger, and bull shark. Today, nets and shark-patrol boats keep away most sharks. During most years, more than 1000 sharks are trapped in the nets. When released, they swim away, as fast as they can.

Oil lighting

Before electricity was invented, lamps were fuelled with shark liver oil. The oil was also used to tan or preserve leather.

The liver of a basking shark has up to a tonne of oil. This is lighter than water, so it helps the fish to float.

Shark repellent

A fish called the Moses sole produces a milky fluid that scares off sharks. For humans, the best idea so far is the POD (Protective Oceanic Device), which can be strapped to a diver's air tank. The battery-powered machine creates an electric field around the diver, which many sharks do not like.

Keep in touch

Since the 1950s, thousands of sharks have been tagged, so that experts can follow their movements. One blue shark was tagged in Britain, and was seen again over a year later 6000 km away, off the coast of Brazil, in South America.

A high-tech tracking method used today is to attach a radio transmitter to a shark's tail. The radio sends a signal to a satellite high up above the Earth. Using information from the satellite, the shark's movements can be mapped for several months, until the radio's batteries run down.

▲ A science team tags a great white shark in the warm waters of 'shark alley', off South Africa.

Skin flap

The eye of some sharks has a flap of skin. This slides over the eye to protect it from harm, especially in the last moments before an attack.

Tasty bite

In 1966, schoolboy Ray Short was swimming in Australia, when a 2m-long great white shark bit his leg. Ray tried to punch its eye, but missed, and instead bit the shark on the nose. Ray survived the attack, and said later that the shark's nose tasted like, 'old, salty canvas'.

Speedy sharks

The fastest shark is thought to be the mako. It has been timed at more than 30 km/h, though only for a short while. Most of the time, it loafs along at about 3 km/h.

▶ Flap of skin slides across the eye like a shutter to protect the shark's eye.

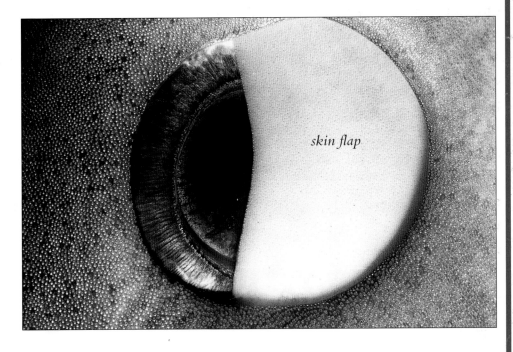

skin flap

SHARK WORDS

Here are some technical terms used in this book.

▲ Diver with anti-shark suit.

anti-shark suit
A diver's over-suit, made of fine metal mesh like a knight's armour. It is worn by divers for protection from shark bites.

cartilage
Gristle – the bendy material from which shark skeletons are made.

denticle
Sharp, tooth-shaped scales that make up a shark's skin. Most fish have scales.

embryo
Any developing animal that is not yet born. In sharks, embryos may develop in the mother, or may be laid in a leathery egg-case, with a yolk for a food supply.

fin
Part of a shark's body used for steering and moving along. The tail fin is also known as the caudal fin. The fins on the back are called dorsal fins, and there are usually two of them.

gill
The body organ that takes oxygen from water. When a shark breathes, water comes in through its mouth, passes over the gills, then out through slits on either side of the body.

lateral line
A line along each side of a shark (and other fish). It gives them the sense of 'distant touch'. A lateral line has many tiny holes, with sensitive hairs inside. These hairs detect small changes in pressure, so a fish

can feel movement of objects or other fish in the water.

liver
The large body organ that helps digest food. It also helps sharks float more easily.

mammal
A warm-blooded animal, such as a human. Mammal mothers feed their young with milk.

mangrove
A tropical tree that has spreading roots. It grows in watery places, and forms a shelter for all sorts of shallow-water creatures, including some species of shark.

parasite
A creature that lives off another. In sharks, parasites

include tapeworms and grubs. They dig in with roots or claws, and suck the shark's blood.

plankton

The general name for all sorts of small sea creatures, from small, shrimp-like animals and baby crabs to fish eggs and worms. Many of these are too small to see without a microscope.

pup

The name for a young shark. A pup may be born live, or hatch out of an egg. A few sharks (including the megamouth) have eggs, but they hatch inside the mother, rather than being laid outside.

remora

A fish that has a free ride on the shark by using a sucker. In return, it helps keep the shark clear of parasites.

species

A group of living things that can breed among themselves. There are more than 350 species in the shark family.

swim bladder

The body organ used by bony fish to control how they float. The bladder swells to let the fish rise. The bladder shrinks to let the fish sink, Sharks have no swim bladder, and sink if they stop swimming. Some sharks have a large, oily liver. Oil is lighter than water, so it helps the shark to float.

▼ The shark uses its fins to steer in water, like an aircraft in the air. The caudal fin acts as a rudder. A slight flex of the pectoral fins angles the shark up or down to swoop or dive.

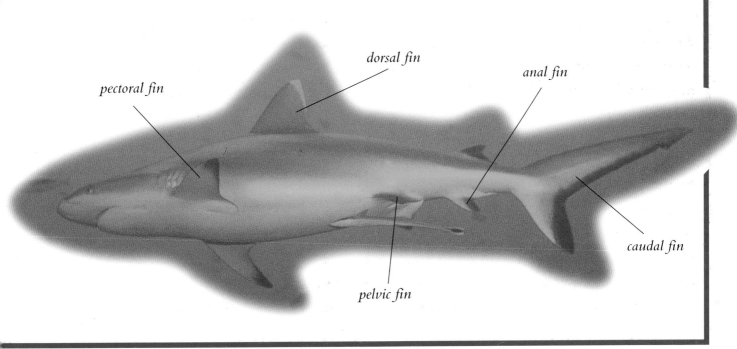

pectoral fin

dorsal fin

anal fin

caudal fin

pelvic fin

SHARK PROJECTS

Making a shark file, with photographs, notes and sketches, will help you find out more about these amazing sea creatures.

◄ You need patience to catch a moving shark with a camera. Don't use flash, as the light may reflect off the aquarium glass. This could spoil your picture, with blobs of white in the middle.

▲ A simple camera can give good results if you are careful.

The best place to see sharks in close-up is at a good oceanarium. Many of these have huge water tanks, in which various undersea creatures swim freely.

Taking photographs is a good way to build up a shark file, though the fish move constantly, and the light is usually poor. Use high-speed film for good pictures.

shark has five gill slits

► Label your photos to show the features of different sharks.

SPEEDING UNDERWATER

A fish such as the great white shark can swim for a time at up to 25 km/h. It has strong muscles for this, but its body shape – long and sleek – helps those muscles work at their best.

This experiment shows you how such a smooth, 'streamlined' shape cuts through the water faster than one that is not so sleek.

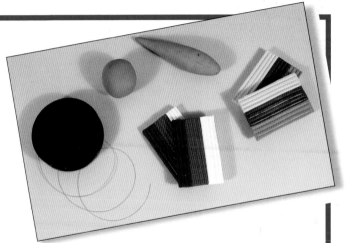

1 You need fishing line, modelling clay and a bowl. Use two 50g pieces of clay to make a ball-shaped fish and a smooth shark shape.

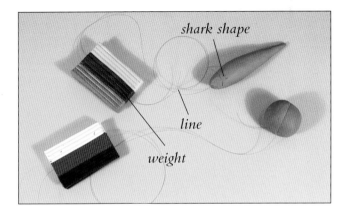

shark shape

line

weight

2 Cut a 90 cm length of line. Squeeze one end into the shark shape, the other into a 60g clay weight. Repeat for the other weight and ball.

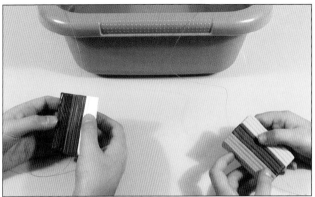

3 Adjust the lines so they are the same length. This should be about 50 cm between fish and weights.

4 Line the fish up at the far end of the bowl, and balance the weights on the near edge. Let the weights drop to see the fish move!

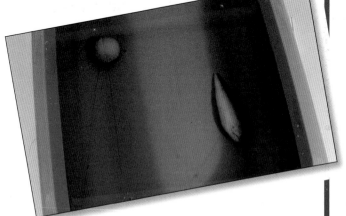

5 Even in a small bowl, the shark should race ahead of the ball – the smooth shark slips through the water very easily.

INDEX